Fractured

Shannon O'Neill

Stairwell Books //

Published by Stairwell Books
161 Lowther Street
York, YO31 7LZ

www.stairwellbooks.co.uk
@stairwellbooks

Fractured © 2021 Shannon O'Neill and Stairwell Books

All rights reserved. No part of this publication may be reproduced, stored in or introduced into a retrieval system, or transmitted, in any form, or by any means (electronic, mechanical, photocopying, recording, e-book or otherwise) without the prior written permission of the author.

The moral rights of the author have been asserted.

Cover Art and illustration by Grace Ireland
Cover and interior design: Alan Gillott

ISBN: 978-1-913432-34-8
P4

Table of Contents

Prologue	1
The Gang	4
Pam I	7
The Cafe	9
Biter	11
Upon Waking Up Face Down in The Gutter With No Memory	12
The Investigation Begins	17
Ferris' Night Off	21
Brightspark	25
Guilt-Trap	26
Who the Fuck Even Is This Guy?	30
Seeking: Reality	32
Mirrors	36
The Cursed	39
Reflections	41
Panoplay I	43
The Decision	52
The First	55
Rebel Girl	57
Good Stories Usually Involve a Wilderness Trip	58
Reactions	62
I Will Take This Potato Chip and Eat It	64
Buttercup	65
Pam II	66
Mother Mary	72
Changing Minds	73
Friendship Insert	75
Looking Glass	77
Panoplay II	78
Traversing the Universe	84
Why	87
Hugging an Alien	90
Prophet	92

Trigger Warning

To my best ability, I have tried to make this work something which discusses mental health and the effects of trauma on the self without explicitly referencing it - more for my sake than yours, quite frankly. This being said, hinting can be heavy, so proceed with caution.

Prologue

Evelyn Marbles sits, doorstep drunk,
southside flat, ankles crossed, tights torn to shreds (as always),
whispering something about gods and prophecies and
always ending thoughts poorly.
Doesn't fear apocalypse, no not since –

> *don't think about it.*

A steady swill.
Witch-brewed potion sloshing against the insides of
her cheeks,
bloated, balloon like. Swallows thrice.
Tongue still tingling and scratches on the inside of her
thigh –

> *don't think about it.*

This is nothing. She is no one,
gone,
barely there to begin with.
Something swallowed, or at least
wishing to be.
She wonders absently if the one who did this even
feels guilty.

> *Doesn't matter.*

Another drink and she'll go in.
The walls seem encroaching now -
she imagines them sprouting mushrooms, Galloway-
esque,

the wicker basket exploding with snakes,
windows crowded with ghosts,
each of their screams turning her skin more acidic.

She doesn't want to but
one more drink and she'll go in.

Because I have to.
Because there is
no other option.

Then comes the shower.
Hot needles of water against the top of her spine,
shivering, wet, frightened but
lathering the soap all the same.
Palm open, palm closed, in you go.
Repetition, ritual. No real difference.

Always waking at witching hour anyway,
nightmare-plagued, melancholy madness.
A hundred interchangeable therapist's faces,
voices blending, scramble suit heads
and the passage of time
crawling forward groggily in the blink of an eye.

Mark me as a target
and I will learn how
to fight.
The pistol cannot
double down on itself,
but I can.

Still resilient.
Still some iron in that gait.
Still some pride left in that spine.
Still something left in here they can't take or break.

She stands in place, motionless monument, for a small eternity,
then stares at the sky.
The stars gaze back with curiosity.

The year passes reluctantly, but it passes all the same. ⁄⁄

The Gang

"Kyle and I met in high school.
Queer kids in small towns always seem to
glob together I guess, tied by their quiet loneliness,
the wide abyss of ignorance always threatening to
take hold of us,
but holding onto each other, well, it made it easier.
Having someone always makes it easier.
It's dead important, that's what my therapist says.
Solidarity. A tangible sense of community
can make even the most grotesque garden green,
so we still keep in touch.
He makes time for me every Saturday,
we drink gin and watch crap tv, fall over laughing
lamenting that the night ever has to end.

Marie's my uni friend.
An intellectual bisexual with a penchant for the
medical.
Yeah, she seems sensible until you get her out, but
there's a *charm*
to being around people when they let their hair down,
isn't there?
I really admire her.
How she always keeps collected,
takes the time to know where her head is,
always funny, empathetic, a real tour de force.

And then, of course, there's Pam.
She's just this girl, you know.
We've been talking for a while.
I think it's something.
I don't want to talk too much in case it isn't, but
I like her.

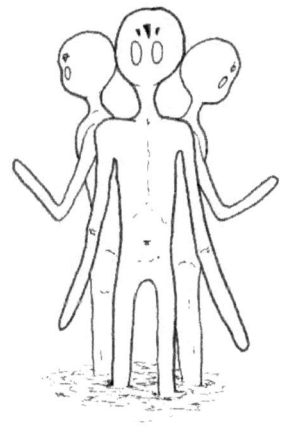

I mean, I really, *really* like her, like
more than butterflies and those telling heart thuds.
She makes my shoulders drop.
My heart hurt less.
I mean, it's probably nothing but, well, I am
a little smitten." ✎

Pam I

I like the way she makes me laugh.
Hides her own secret smirks under quizzical
eyebrows,
elaborate punnery paired with the gutter perfectly.
The fountain of knowledge that seems to spring so
carelessly, carefully-poured-over pages related
effortlessly.
She is a sponge of information, soaks in everything.
I'm an engine - only take what I need to get by.
She has the softest sigh.
Chin in the palm of her hand, sort of
dreamy-eyed.
There are star clusters in them, I'm sure of it.
I'd follow her into oblivion frankly any day of the
week.

When she kisses my cheek,
it's like unicorns are real,
all the love songs make sense,
I *finally* understand why people like marmalade.

Have you ever had a kiss like that?
Even
just
one?

I think the phrase they use is
'life changing.'

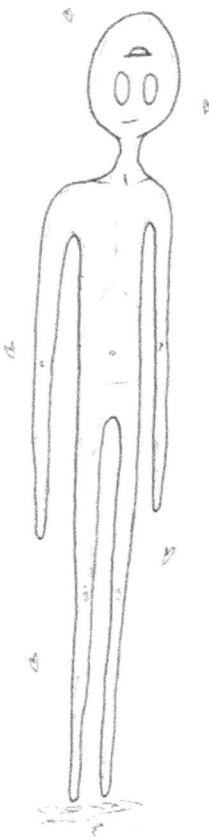

The Cafe
(Hi hello, though not explicit, this one might be lightly triggering.
Implied sexual aggressiveness/intention of assault)

No one knows how he got in.
Thought she'd locked the door when she took the bins out, but
closing was so *busy* you see,
and she wanted to get out early, she's got a date tonight and well,
she just wanted to look pretty.
Get home quickly. Shower.
Maybe dress up a bit.
Pam's special, she thinks,
and it's not unhealthy to want to impress her.
Probably. Anyway.

None of that matters now.

He's big.
Much, *much* bigger than her,
growing larger, ogre-like,
his teeth grow tusks, his mouth drips blood,
obscured by the chaos of thought, he keeps talking, drooling,
she swears saliva turns to blood when it hits the ground.
Transfixed and quiet, she stares,
head too crowded to think in this
deafening silence.

I know danger and it looks
just like this.

Her eyes count exit strategies.

Her knees tremble, the gravity too fierce a force to fight.
Outside, flickering streetlights and the absence of anyone passing by.
Pats her pockets, then hands retreat to her side, empty.

Phone in her bag. Alarm in the back.
Nothing useful or with which to dodge this attack.
Wishes she'd *ever* gotten around to those self-defence classes.
But things were busy. Life got harder to manage.
She couldn't leave the house for *months*.

It is at this point that he pulls out the metaphorical gun.

The world drops out from under her. ⫽

Biter

You think you're a monster but I am an eternal destruction.

They used to sing songs of me as scarlet bled into stone,
as fish died in the river, as the thread of fate was cut.
My temples were sacrifice, shattered plates and broken bones.
Never needed a banshee to tell me who'd die next.
So.
Careful what you make of your next step.

I've got hands they call world-eaters.
Palms that crush cities to sand.
I am the fall of Rome incarnate,
the reason the word terror even exists on your tongue.
See, only the small demons need to clench their fists, young one.
I hold power in a simple flick of the wrist.

Watch and see. ◢

Upon Waking Up Face Down in The Gutter with No Memory

Oh shit.
Oh shit. Oh shit. Oh shit oh shit oh *shit*.

Where am I?
What happened?
What are these marks?
What did I *do?*

I remember anger, so much anger, and then–

Keep calm. Sit up.
Get a hold of yourself.
Take a breath.

What do you remember?
Not much. His entrance, my rage,
a feeling like extra teeth forcing up through my gums,
then

darkness, blackout, waking up
here. Wherever here is.
Nothing else.

Fuck, did I–
No. 'Course not. Don't be silly.
I'm not a killer.
Of course I'm not a killer.
I am centred, I am calm, I am
something of a misconstruction,
shambles of a girl, but
certainly
not a killer.

I don't remember.
Why don't I remember?
Just his vinegar breath, the way he reached for my
neck, then
fade to black.

Where am I?
There are
stamps on my arm, small triangles encircled,
and I don't remember *anything*.

This is what trauma does to the brain, I know that,
but

god, did I *kill* him?

That would be the logical presumption.
Blood on my clothes, bruises on my arms.
Signs of a struggle, but nothing but
surface cuts.
I'm not a killer.
I *know* I'm not a killer.
Not a monster.
Not one of them.

                But I don't really know that.
                No one really knows that, do they?
                Shit Ev, existential nausea won't help
                here or anywhere. Stand up.
                Get it *together*.

Bearings.
I need *bearings*.
Left looks familiar, right much more so.

Follow the footsteps of my history.
I see a church in the distance.
Memories tap me on the shoulder and wait patiently.

I used to come here.
Every Sunday, like clockwork.
Prettiest dresses, hands scrubbed clean,
those precious rosary beads.

Not for a long time though.

Weird, you know?
Looking at pieces of the past that don't fit anymore,
parts of you gone, dismantled, unravelled.
I used to believe in god and well, not anymore.
I like to try and focus on history now,
the continuous human story,
think it's mad and wonderful how it all
fits in and somehow doesn't.
Shit, my cousin's pious as hell, hope she isn't here.
Is it Sunday? What's the time?
I wouldn't reckon but–

> *I*
> *might've killed*
> *someone.*

Shit. Forgot about that for a second.
In a church of all places.
Probably bad. Definitely a sin.
I don't believe in sins or anything anymore, but
I hope I haven't committed a big one.

Maybe he tried to kill me.
Maybe that's why I woke up like this,
with a half panicked heart and these bruised wrists.

Maybe that's why I attacked him back.
Who knows?

Oh,
this is nonsense anyway.
Rubbish. Absolute shite.
I don't even remember, and I'm not
a killer, I'm not, I'm not–

But I might be.
and that speculation haunts me.
Sinks into my skin.
Turns my stomach upside down, pancake flip.

I need to know
what happened,
whose blood this is.

There's no sense of direction if you don't even know
what you're driving. ⫽

The Investigation Begins

I take a few days off work
   (it's alright, boss quite likes me, her name is Magrat
      and she saves me cake on Wednesdays)
and the investigation starts film noir style.

By which I mean,
I spend a lot of the morning monologuing to myself.

Watch the way the light splinters,
small slivers of silver through purple curtains creates
kaleidoscope across my carpet
and I let my fingers linger in it,
skin turned shades that makes me think of mermaids,
and I
forget myself a minute.

Just a minute.
It's always so brief, this blessing,
impermanent relief from the mess my head's in,
but at least I can find it here.

Some aren't so lucky.

I know how loud the screaming gets if you don't know
how to drown it out,
and myself, I forget my methods often, so I try not to
judge them,
only want to hug them harder–

Shit.
I forgot I might be a murderer.

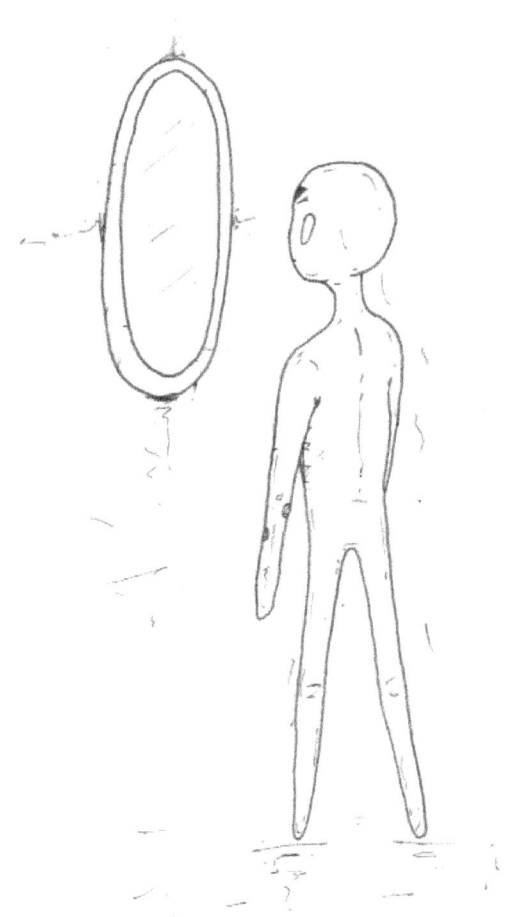

Don't know why that won't stick.
Like overused blue-tac limp against plaster,
the notion is reluctant to remain.
I am *praying* this is a good sign,
but I don't *know* anything.

Hope my empathy has carried me but without
memory,
how am I to know?

I start planning things out.
Writing them down.
Make sketches of his face (without tusks this time)
and try and recall the way his voice groaned
but the memory shakes me to my very bones and it is
a struggle to recall anything at all these days,
so crowded am I in my mind's own miseries.
I collate the evidence regardless.
Head down, have to focus.
What do we know so far?

Woke up, no memory, next to a car
two train stops away, three hours gone,
stamps on my arm and bruises and
well,
blood.
Think it's mostly mine from all the small cuts and
scratches but if I'm honest,
there's a lot more than would be expected, and I
just can't be sure.

Who was that guy?

Try the internet.
Google and Facebook dive with nothing to go on.
Nothing. Unsurprising.

Keep looking. Have to find something.
Drink more coffee. Smoke a cigarette.
Who likes the cafe?
Forty people. Not much.
Unlikely. Still searching,
and then

like the universe singing a sickly rainbow into
existence, I spot his likeness, image
staring dead-eyed smile over a poker table.
Friend of a friend.
It makes my skin crawl.
Still, that's him.
Unmistakable.

I swallow the bile rising in my throat and click the
profile. ⁄⁄

Ferris' Night Off

It's too easy.
Of *course* it's too easy.
Must be a trap.
Must be a set up.
Can't just be *this*.

But maybe it is.
Maybe it's just coincidence
one of our mutual friends was having a party tonight,
round the corner, and I'm invited.

Not like we're close or anything.
Just an old teenage friend kind of thing, but it's one of
those big hall parties, you know,
where you invite everybody
just to fill up the room.

I turn up around nine, buy some wine and settle in.

Ferris is the birthday boy, twenty five,
reclining against a red leather sofa with that cocky
smile he's had since high school,
looking to the world like a king surveying his town,
but I know he's softer.
We used to get together sometimes just to out-hope
the winter.
It's been a while so when I say hi, he seems surprised
and I can see the way his eyes light up to greet me.

> It'd be nicer to be remembered fondly
> if I didn't already feel like a
> ghost all the time.

We start chatting.
There's the catch up and mentioning break ups,
'whereabout do you live now,' you know, just
standard. We pitter patter around the names of friends we've
both stopped talking to or about for various reasons
and pretend we didn't fuck that awful time we went
camping.
He mentions a friend's gone missing and says that
dreaded name.

I see it flash across my vision, black and white typing,
hold my breath.
Fuck
fuck
fuck.

This is confirmation.
This is damnation, theory solidification,
I mean, he says he hasn't seen him in a few days,
that's all,
but...

I don't know.
I don't know I don't know *I don't know*.
Shit. I can't think. My head
is a hornet nest and my skin is burning.
I don't know what's happening.
I'm thirsty. I'm so *thirsty*.
He's still talking and I
don't know if I'm a monster
or not. It's too loud. I can't think.

I don't know what to *do*.

Just stop thinking.
Just keep drinking.
Drown it out.
Don't panic. Act normal.
Make an excuse.
Go home.
Go home go home go home.
Deal with this
tomorrow.

The world falls out from under me again. ◢

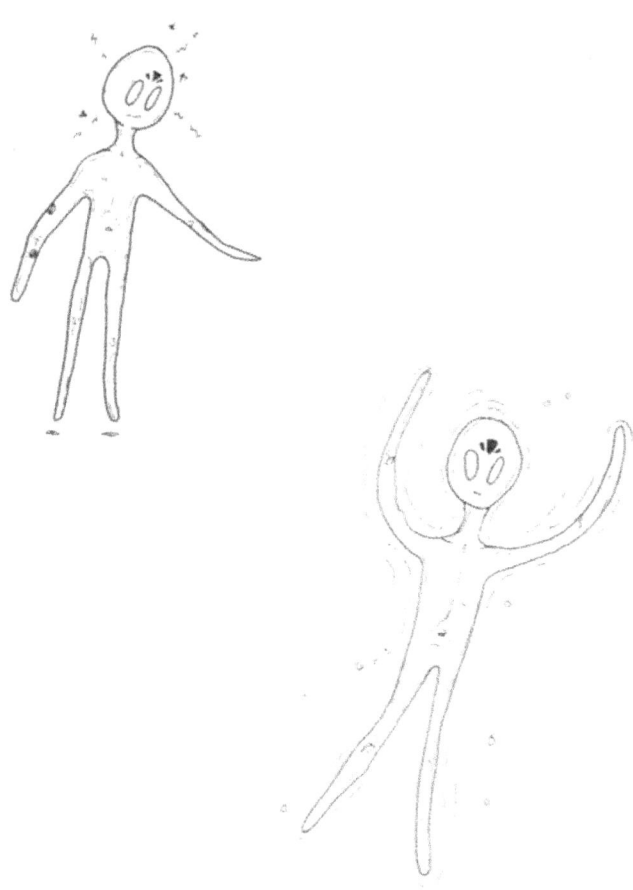

Brightspark

Burn the ashes, scorch the earth,
my body's craving blood and mirth,
I'm trampled in the afterbirth
and tangled, strangled, sick with hurt.
This thirst for anger, what's it worth?
A burst of panic quickly curved.
I serve the converts quite the scourge,
divert the factions to a purge.
Confer with demons, vision blurred,
I'm mixing potions, drink the curse,
and wondering what I deserve
while coming up and quite disturbed.
I'm making hearses out of bottles,
floor it then I grab the throttle,
I am no apostle, often awful,
self-destructive model.

These doors are menacing
and I still fear this beckoning.
Daylight seems so threatening.
This madness just keeps meddling.
The whiskey isn't settling.
Now morning comes with reckoning,
and psychologic levelling,
tonight is just for deadening
and revelling the hell we've made.
I wanna make a new mistake.
Knees, remember how to shake,
surrender to the soulless rave.
Dismember til my heart's awake.
Adventure in forgotten graves.
Inventor of the parting gaze,
but never liked the aftertaste.

Guilt-Trap

I do not feel like me right now.

Like a sickness has swam into me and broken all my bones,
sliced the skin and let all my sweetness out.
I can't hold anything down.
Toilet bowl marked with attempt after attempt but nothing,
even the water knows I'm wrong and if I sleep, it's never for long.
Nightmare-riddled, guilt tripping up my tongue,
I sober up staggering through my livingroom.

I don't know what happened, but the boy from the cafe is gone
and I woke up with blood I still haven't washed out my clothes,
and those things seem too connected to really be put to chance.

I don't know how to react.
Think distantly I should call a psychiatrist, the police, at least a friend
but none of this makes any sense and I am worried that they'd just lock me up.

Maybe they should.
Maybe I'm dangerous.
My own skin tells me I'm dangerous daily,
maybe it's right. Maybe I'm—

Shut up. You don't know anything for certain.

I wake up around three. Spend the following five
hours staring at a wall, decide
if nothing else, I should go to class, don't know why,
think
normality's just compelling now.
Grab my bag, my bundle of pens, three dog-eared
books.

Oh god, I *killed* someone.

Don't think about it.

Just breathe.
Go to class. Do something normal.
If it still seems real in a few hours,
we go to the police, do the right thing,
protect the world.

I just wanted to help. All I've ever wanted to do is
help.
I don't know how this happened.

The hall is crowded.
The lecture's in this architectural marvel by the river
with pillars and new glass walls,
I take a seat near the middle and try to disappear
as always, though admittedly with more force this
time.

It doesn't work.
Marie spots me from across the room and comes
bounding,
coloured gel pens and grins, asks how I am and I
concoct a lie that sounds like 'yeah I'm fine,'
she mentions a friend is coming but I've already
stopped listening.

I've *killed* someone.
And I know it's not the *point* or anything and there
are much bigger concerns,
but I *hate* myself right now,
burning rage and desire to eye gouge.
Everything warm that comes toward me feels like
poison in my mouth.
Marie means well, but well,
that's the problem.

I'm having trouble staying stuck in reality
and she's only sweetly cause she doesn't know what
I've done.
I've *killed* someone.

How could I do that?
Even if he hurt me, even if he tried first,
how could I *do* that?

I am no god, I do not make these calls.

I want to vomit.
I want to vomit but it is sticking in my throat, a small
plague of its own,
a million locusts.
I don't know where the floor is.
I don't feel like I can breathe.

Marie taps me lightly on the shoulder and I heave a
little,
pass it off as just feeling sickly.
Not untrue.

When the lecturer, Giovanni, enters the room the
lights dim, the presentation begins, there is some

shuffling behind me and Marie says hello to someone
so I turn, curious,

and meet eyes with the man I thought I'd murdered. ⧘

Who the Fuck Even Is This Guy?

He's still tall, but different.
Seems to shrink into that blue plastic chair sort of sheepishly,
one hand in his pocket, the other jotting things down clumsily
like the pen is unfamiliar in his hand.
As the lecture ends, he stands to go
and I am struck motionless,
frozen, electric chair rigid -
I've only seen it in movies,
a body's betrayal.

Watch distantly as Marie makes brief conversation
and I am trying not to listen, but I'm
not really in a position *not* to be, I mean

He stands there like he's done nothing wrong
and he speaks so gently, much calmer than before,
shoves his hands in his pockets,
gives the impression of soft, meek, harmless
and I just don't trust it.

He says he's new. To this course anyway, had a sort of epiphany, something just came together, a change of heart.
Felt he had to play some part in making the world a better place,
a sudden awareness of his position in time and space
that led him, well,
I guess here.

Bullshit.
Made up.
Move on.

Marie tugs my arm.
The man from the cafe smiles at me but it seems
splintered somehow,
unnatural on his face.
Of course I think the worst.
My hands begin to shake,
small trembles I can hide in fidgets,
pen clicked, unclicked, then

he says something.
It's insignificant really, a normal turn of phrase,
maybe a reaction to

                              don't think about it.

But it sticks to me somehow.
Makes a hammering in my chest,
pulls something in me up,
alert, aware.

"I feel like a different person," he says, just
sort of standing there.

So I look at him. I mean, I *really* look at him,
forget the fear of awkward eye contact, I mean I *stare*,
devouring his everything, trying to get a hold on
whatever this is.

Because he might be right.
He carries himself, gestures, walks
a little differently, the same but somehow
altered, and I might be mad but it feels
like it has something to do with me.

How can that be? ⁄⁄

Seeking: Reality

I don't know what to believe.
Skin still tingling with this energy and a lightning rod
inside of me, yet there's no clear path to send this
flame.
Am I going insane?
Hardly be the first time but that line of thinking only
gets you so far–
what about the scars on my arm, the purple bruises,
all that blood?
I didn't just make those up.
I washed it all out in the sink, cold water,
it turned the liquid blushing pink.
I remember it
with crystal clear clarity.

I tried talking to Marie but she's all platitudes lately,
and Kyle is busy, Pam
hasn't talked to me in days.
I stood her up, haven't explained why.
I don't know *how* to explain why.
I might be losing my mind, or maybe something
far more sinister.

I don't remember and the puzzle pieces still haven't
slotted into–

Hold on.
I'm missing something.
Something important, I can feel it.
Crucial clues trapped
on the tip of my tongue.
My brain just hasn't caught up yet.
I need to think.
Take a moment, trust my instincts–

Fuck this, I just wanna *dance*.
Slide my hands up thigh skin, smooth rhythms, lose myself in that bassline.
Pounding, guttural, abandon you can hold onto, lap up the electric energy, movement, let it utterly consume me.
I wanna fuck.
I wanna feel.
I wanna dance until the world comes crumbling and ashes drown me.
I wanna go out *happy*.
But mostly, I just wanna go out.
Can't stand it here right now.
Feel too restless, god I wish this sudden deathwish didn't come with such confusion.
My body doesn't feel much for moving but I'll sort that out,
few cans down my mouth, no bother–

Keep your *focus* Ev.
Try to remember the gutter.
Waking up. No memory.
Lights like lucid dreaming, blood on my hand, stamps on my–

Stamps.
Small triangles encircled, what looked like paint but had stuck to skin with more defiance,
looked familiar, reminded me of Ryan and that club we used to go to,
what was it called?
Shut down years ago.
That place in the corner of town no-one talks about, where I used to let the melody slice me in half.

But there's something about it.
That building, pile of ruin, I can't place it.
A stir in the brickwork, loud, dramatic thrum.

My feet move.
Lock the door, down the stairs.
Shuffle down backstreets and under streetlights,
quick pace,
find themselves near central, push on further, then
there it is.
Great detritus of mismatched heritage in collapsing
stone,
a doorway that somehow feels like home
but I haven't been here in years.

And this place is dead. Buried. I've seen more lively
corpses.
I am standing in a boneyard, there are
no answers here, there is no answer, I'm just going
mad,
I must be, I must be, I must be.

Mirrors

The clock strikes three.
Pools of gold spill out the windows, blossoms on the
ledge begin to bloom,
and the door swings open softly, without sound.
There is a beckoning.
I follow it, unblinking, not knowing why or who is
pulling,
feet still following their own forgotten tune

and the room smells like burnt sage,
a hall of mirrors and smoke tendrils,
empty but the roses, thornless, atop a nearby desk
and the globe in the centre of the room.
It is waist high, golden, glittering but grim,
relic of decadence, a sparkling kind of grunt.

"Not to be blunt, but are you the girl who was
supposed to come?"

I jump.
Pivots on my heel, electrified with terror, meets the
face of
well, someone,
tall, lanky, covered in shadows,
a silhouette.

"Oh sorry," he says. "We've already met.
You can just go on right ahead."

He gestures left.
I follow his hand, mounting terror, stomach ache,
walk in silence through the corridor, then left again,
This is dangerous

down some stairs,
What am I doing?
through that door and
the carnival unravels before me.

Silks and streamers, lanterns and lights,
colours dancing across skin and the sway of the crowd
so inviting,
perhaps fifty bodies in time, dashing one step to the
next, it feels
just like magic, have to catch it.
Jaw slack, I watch wide-eyed,
entranced.

Then comes the end of the dance,
a habitual lazy shrug,
dispersing crowd, scattered footsteps,
and the woman standing alone in the centre, she is
ageless.

She is Alice, she says.
First of the Cursed,
a woman who speaks of chaos raging through the
centuries.
She says this place is refuge, sanctuary
for those who exist, like her, as something else.

I guess now *I* exist as something else. ⌗

The Cursed

They are caught fabric on the fence of the universe.
Stories forgotten to be scrubbed clean, vivid lives
which have yet evaded all detection.
I listen to them endlessly, hungrily,
bite chunks out of their narrative,
throw back the chaser of my own,
drink them all in.

Aside from Alice, there is Anna,
tall woman cloaked in green.
She reminds me of my mother with all that old pain in
her eyes.
She has the ability to manipulate time,
"although, you know, only selectively."
Spends her time darting in and out of memories,
relishing the time she has left with long buried sons.

Fin is the brightest one. He tells me
beyond the history of the place, things he couldn't
possibly know, like
which nights I used to go here, with whom. It's
alarming.
Alice says *"stop trying to be charming, Fin, the girl
needs solid facts,"*
so we get back to that. Says his knowledge is
limited, leaves when he does a given space. .

(I start to notice every gift comes with a restraint,
so what is mine?)

We move down the line.
Fifty faces introduced in quick succession,
I meet the doorman who makes hand-sized portals,

the painter whose works come to still life,
each story echoing remnants of my own.
The blackouts, the dread, not remembering this place.
It all begins to make sense -
or at least, some semblance of it.

Alice stands with the energy of a preacher in a pulpit.
I approach her as the crowd begins to spill out.
I lay out my questions, she replies "I can't answer them,
but I can show you how to." ⧸⧸

Reflections

Alice takes me to the side.
"Are you sure you want to know?"
It's why I came.
"You might not like all that you see."
I have to know it.
"Alright. You have a right to, I suppose."
She digs deep in her pocket.
"Hold this."
I take it, run my thumb across the stone's edge,
nodding softly, bated breath.
I don't know what's happening, I just hope
that this holds an answer.

She turns me towards the mirror.
Straightens my shoulders.
Says to watch the reflection, how it moves,
and so I do.
I watch it for what feels like hours. I just
stand there, watching,
my limbs aching, staring until my eyes sting,
until my body is begging for movement,
until I am sure this is not some endless dream.

Because I see what she means.
The *moment* I look, I see them staring back,
a scramble suit slowly unfurling.
They all look like me.

Different though.
One carries herself taller, glasses, flowery air and
gentle charm,
another leans on her shoulder almost desperately.
The third is quiet violence, seething eyes.

while the fourth will not look directly at me.
The fifth leans back, crossed legged on a barrel, lights a cigarette and gently waves.
The sixth keeps giggling, bubbling champagne laughter,
and the last, she just keeps scribbling.

"So," I say, "these are the other parts of me."

The last rears her head, indignant. "Well. Not exactly." //

Panoplay I

Lauren: We are a product *of* you, but we are not necessarily, exactly, *you*. You're just... tied to us, or at least our universe is tied to *you* somehow. It's rather difficult to grasp, actually, but my best theory so far is that it's linked to your panic responses – fear, rapid heartbeat–

Brightspark: I doubt she wants the whole spiel.

Evelyn: Oh but I think I *do*.

Rebel Girl: You really don't. *[She shakes her head]* And we don't have the time anyway.

Evelyn: I came here for answers.

Rebel Girl: And you'll get them, but this place disappears into another dimension in around ten minutes.

Evelyn: How do you know that? *I* don't even know that.

[Rebel Girl shrugs]

Rebel Girl: Maybe you do, maybe you don't. Maybe part of you was listening, maybe I'm a wholly different entity. Why does it matter?

Evelyn: *I* think it matters! You've been, you've been taking over my body, doing god knows what with it—

Brightspark: Oh, relax. All we did was keep you safe. Take you home.

Mother Mary: Yes, we'd never hurt you, dear. We only want what's *best* for you.

Evelyn: How can I trust that? I don't even know who you—

Biter: You're us, we're *you*, except we're in a different micro dimension or something. Keep up, cuntface.

Evelyn: But how? Who are you? How does that work? It doesn't even make… How do I get rid of it?

Prophet: Those aren't the kind of questions you should be asking.

Buttercup: Don't you like us, Evelyn?

Biter: 'Course she doesn't.
And we don't like her either, ungrateful piece of—

Evelyn: *[angry]* What the *hell* is your problem?

Biter: You are! We fucking saved you from that—

Evelyn: *By taking over my body!* Do you know how invasive–

Brightspark: Now, now, there's no need to–

Lauren: If you'd just let me explain in the first place–

Buttercup: **Quiet.**

[Buttercup's wail is a deafening whisper. The group falls silent]

Buttercup: We're running out of time.

Lauren: She's right.

Evelyn: I'll cut to the chase then. The blackouts, do you know why they're happening? Is it... is that you?

Lauren: Yes. No. Sort of. It's... When your heart rate quickens and you seem to be under extreme psychological distress, that's when our 'pocket' universe and your sense of reality sort of, well, collapse into each other. Sometimes there's an event, an aggressor, sometimes–

Evelyn: Sometimes I just panic. Right. Got it. [*She thinks*] Okay. We'll come back to that one. What about... ah, shit, what was his name? The, you

	know... the guy. What happened to him?
Lauren:	We may have... tweaked a few things.
Brightspark:	Nothing bad.
Buttercup:	We made him better.
Evelyn:	'Better' how? And how did you, you know, do it?
Lauren:	Well, we're um, we're not really sure, and um...
Evelyn:	*Jesus.* Do you people have *any* answers?

[Lauren frowns, grows a little hot-headed]

Lauren:	I'm the *only* ambiguously scientific *being* in a pocket universe physically limited by your internal life. *I* think I'm doing just fine, given what I'm working with. *[Then, softer, regretful]* Sorry, I just mean that, well, in order to give you the answers you need, I'd have to, um, well...
Biter:	We need you to do it again.
Evelyn:	*What?*
Lauren:	We'd, um, we'd need more

	case data. More subjects to study. A few controlled studies too, certainly, but–
Evelyn:	I'm not doing *anything* until you explain what you're doing to these people.
Biter:	And *she's* telling *you* she doesn't know because it's not exactly fucking voluntary, shit for brains. Fucking *listen* sometimes, eh.
Rebel Girl:	She's not wrong. It's less control, more codependency. When you're in distress, our entire reality shudders, alters somehow, and when we put the pieces back together, then there's... the *effect* on whoever's around. Increased empathy, altered perception, more grounded sense of self. It's not like we're *hurting* anyone.
Brightspark:	Yeah. It's like... permanent mdma for the personality.
Mother Mary:	Don't say that.
Lauren:	Please don't. It's *highly* inaccurate...
Rebel Girl:	It's more like an, ah, antivirus maybe? Once the threatening parts of the personality are detected, they're zoned in on,

	quarantined and, well, eliminated. We *think*.
Evelyn:	That doesn't sound sinister at *all*.
Lauren:	Well, jesus, we're not happy about this either. I didn't curse *myself* into existence.
Mother Mary:	Time, dear.
Lauren:	Right, right. Evelyn, I, um, *we* need you to... to try and do it again. Change someone. Don't look at me like that, I know I *know*. But it's the only way to figure any of this out. More data, cases to study. By activating it, we run the best chance of learning to control it, maybe even mitigate its effect on us and the people in your world.
Evelyn:	What about the data you have? Can't you do something with that?
Lauren:	The first time, we didn't, we didn't even know what was happening, and the second, well, I've learned all I can, but–
Evelyn: *[alarmed]*	Second case?
Biter:	Aye, you remember. That wank outside Ferris'. Kept making fun of his girlfriend, even after she started crying. Did a bit of, you

	know, rewiring. *[She makes a snipping motion with her fingers]*
Brightspark:	Close proximity. Wrong place wrong time.
Evelyn:	No, I don't remember, because someone keeps–
Rebel Girl:	Stealing your body, *we get it*. Not voluntarily. No one here is against you. We're *all* trying to figure out what's happening and stop it as best we can. *Relax* a little, will you? *[She inhales]* Hopefully now you're aware of what's happening, the memory thing will fix itself. That's what Anna said, isn't it? That once she knew what it was, her memory started to recover.
Evelyn:	Did she say that? I'm still so–
Prophet:	Time's up.
Evelyn:	–confused. Wait. No. No, I need more time. I still have questions, I need answers. Can't you just–
Rebel Girl:	It's almost sunrise and this place disappears before the first normal human steps foot on the street. Precautionary measure. And you can't be here when it does, or you'll end up a thousand miles away with no means to get home except

	waiting until this place maybe, *maybe*, lands here again. Which it won't unless someone outside wants it to.
Evelyn:	How do you know *that*? *I* didn't–
	[Rebel Girl shrugs]
Rebel Girl:	Suspension of disbelief, Ev. Just go with it. ✏

The Decision

One world drops out from under me, the other swims into view
and I am awash with the wetness of both,
somehow drifting,
somehow floating,
somehow sinking like a rock.
I feel my feet against riverbed, then
I am returned.

Alice steadies me by the shoulders.
Her soft voice over the crackle of the fire, soothing.
Someone offers me a drink.
I gulp it, down the hatch, singe of ethanol on my tongue, ice on my teeth,
spare a glance at the mirror, it is
empty.

I ask, "Be honest, am I going crazy?"

Alice says "Maybe,
but that isn't what this is."

I say, "Okay.
I have to think."
Roll my sleeves up to the elbow,
sit cross-legged on the ground,
ask *anyone* to get me some paper.
I make a list. Keep glancing at my mirror image but it remains vacant–

well,
I mean,
there's still
me.

Funny to look at now.
Knowing what's underneath, just
below the reflection.

Come on, focus.
The sun is coming up.

Pros and cons. Those work, seem
simple. I could do with a little simple right now.

Pros	Cons
Attains data we need.	Ethically dubious
Not as ethically dubious as it could be	<– that's not really a pro
Minimises harm	Playing god. Not advisable. See: all of history
I have superpowers	<– also not technically a pro.

Could help people in some small
marginal way if I control it, learn to
command it, master all the...
weird.
And I guess it might reduce my daily fear or
something.

I don't feel good about this but fuck it, well, alright, I'll
try.

Gotta trust your selves sometime or another,
right? ⁄⁄

The First

I'm wavering already.
Eyeing up the guy across the street, he's been
shouting at that poor boy for
hours now, screaming bloody murder.
I've been watching,
unblinking,
and it's *awful*,
but I don't know that he deserves *this*.

I think back to my mirror image, feel the heaviness
of spark under my skin.

I don't feel good about doing this, but I
think I have to.
It'll come out somehow anyway, won't it?
Get utilitarian about it.
Vic for the maximum amount of happiness.

A train skitters across the bridge and the city
shudders at night
but that doesn't bother me anymore. Feels familiar.
I too am something grit and grime and pearls, a
thriving ecosystem with crumbling skyscrapers
abound.
I feel its heartbeat
deep inside me.
Look up.

The guy slams the door shut.
Leaves the boy crying, cleaning up glass,
and my stomach drops at that.
With grim resolve, I walk toward the door.

I do not know how I do it.
A tap on the shoulder. Somehow
atoms realigning, and the shadows drift out of his
eyes.
I watch them work.
I do not know how they do it.
Seven shifting figures all about him,
growling or crooning, gentle and grim.
Ghoulish and yet so serene.
His shoulders drop.
They motion for me to move and for whatever reason I do,
feel the wind compel my body to bend
this way and that, contorting my back,
a primal energy coursing through me.

They leave the scent of strawberries and a pale gold
dust in their wake.

The stranger shakes his head. Blinks twice, confused,
and suddenly there are bruises on my arm.

Ah. So that's where those come from.

He blinks a third time, eyelash half-moons pressed
against cheek,
Exhales, says "Oh, come in out of the street.
It'll rain soon, wouldn't want you to get wet."

I thank him, say, "But it's not raining yet
and I'm afraid I have other places to be." ⫽

Rebel Girl

I'm gonna change the world, baby.
Just sit back and watch me.
I am a reckoning. So far from sedentary
when you see me next rest,
it'll be in the cemetery.
I walk the route of this apocalypse so gently for
someone only born yesterday,
don't you think?

Sit down.
Take a drink,
a smoke, a breath.
Watch me carve this warpath, tear open pavements
where the bodies they broke came back.
We're not just hunting,
we're a haunting now.
You and me, we're going to *make* them listen.
Some drumbeats you just can't ignore.

And when it's burnt down to the bannisters,
when we've taken all their weapons,
melted their metals, turned them into tools,
then we can build our new world.
Forget how to turn bodies into battalions,
clean your torn up knees with alcohol,
teach the children something other than how to suffer.

It's so simple. Just a puzzle to solve.
And now, finally, the key.

I'm going to fix it.
Everything has been waiting for me to fix it, and I'm
here now.
Where else would I possibly be?

Good Stories Usually Involve a Wilderness Trip

Under tarpaulin skies, we lie,
our heads pressed together like some indie film cover,
pastel lit,
three scraggly, bruised-knees twenty somethings
searching the sky for promise
desperately.
I start to scratch my knees incessantly.
Kyle notices.
He always does.

He asks "What's up?"
and I want to tell him but it sounds crazy,
I want to tell them but I'm sure they'll reject me,
I want to tell them but I'm scared that it might be real.

I whittle it down, carve my heart until it's smaller, pocket sized,
something that others can swallow.

I say "I do not feel very stable right now," and he touches my hand, gives me those soft eyes, furrowed brows.

"Then talk to us."

And I want to.
God I want to.
But it is stuck to my stomach, immovable,
a sunken stone,
and they won't understand,
can't understand.

Even *I* don't understand so
how could they?

I wonder why god made me this way then remember I
don't believe in him anymore.

I shuffle back, emotionally retract, pick a
smaller sadness.

"Pam still hasn't texted back."

I know my friends too well.
Knew they'd reply with soft sighs and hugs,
rationalisations and love,
but they respect me too much to pry further.

"Do you ever wonder," I continue unsurely,
weighted tongue, bile heavy throat,
"what it'd be like to have the power to change the
world?
And I mean, *really* change it.
Somehow know the secret, how to
break people down to their smallest components and
then
build them back up stronger,
kinder, more able to accept each other?
I mean, if you could, you would,
wouldn't you?"

Marie's twinkling laugh. She wipes her lip, blinks.
"I mean of course. Wouldn't you say that almost
everyone has?
It's just a basic saviour complex,
see a problem, want to fix it, but
it's not like it's a one step two step process.

This impossible dream of consciousness, we don't
realistically
know enough about it, how we got here, what we're
here for, what's our...
purpose–"

"But if you could?" Kyle asks.

She nods. "Of *course* I would,
but how would anyone even *do* that?"

I stifle nervous laughs.
Swallow them with a swig, tell myself the bile makes
it a cocktail,
smile, relax, you're safe, and anyway
doesn't this mean I did the right thing?
You see,
the spin of the earth has seemed so dizzy lately
but at least I got the right direction.
Right?
The moral purpose,
my place as protagonist, I am
doing good I think, at least
I hope.

I wanna be a hero in the story if I can, you know.

"Do you really mean that?" I ask, finishing the glass.
"If you could, you would, wouldn't you? Obviously."
I try to mitigate the lump in my throat with awkward
comedy.

"Ev, you've got a weird tone."

I nod. "I know."
Press lips to fingertips,

heartbeat in my stomach cacophony.
I can see moonlight through the plastic window,
It, like me, is shivering.
I know now why the wolves all howl at it.

"Ev, are you okay?"
Kyle knocks over his shoe on the way toward me, it
goes skittering under the door.
He pays it little mind.

I have underestimated them.
Thought I knew them enough to outrun them,
forgetting
they know all of my best steps too. I say
"It's been confusing lately and I don't know what to
do."

Marie says tell us about it,
and for whatever reason
I do. ⁄⁄

Reactions

"Wait. Are you serious?"
Marie looks quite delirious.
Kyle looks downright confused.
And I am worried I have spoiled the good mood.

"Unfortunately so."
Their eyebrows furrow.
I shuffle awkwardly - no other way to do it.
Fill my cup, down in one, look at my friends.

"Well, I guess," Kyle begins, holding his head,
"this is a fair bit to take in. I might actually need a minute."
I pat his shoulder. He smiles gently.
I feel... okay.

"And I've got questions," interjects Marie,
caught somewhere between wonder and glee.
"I mean, you know, if it's alright to ask."

"I'll answer what I can,
but honestly, it's still a mystery to me -
I've got people working on it though.
Hopefully have some answers soon.
Honestly, I'd just like to be rid of it."

"Don't be so fucking stupid."
Kyle's boom catches us off guard.
He never shouts. Hasn't since we were fourteen.
He apologises profusely.
Says he doesn't really know where that came from.
"But to throw away this opportunity, it seems to me

a waste, I mean, the universe has conspired to help you out.
Doesn't that sound like some kind of call to adventure?"

I think about this too much later, staring at the sky. ◢

I Will Take This Potato Chip and Eat It

I am righteous now.
Finally filled with purpose.
I am the priestess, this my ritual,
watch me alter the earth's very core.
I do it only in your best interest.

I mean.
This isn't so bad now, is it?
Much calmer, don't you think?
Those guys at college leave Kyle alone.
Marie's tutor isn't an arsehole
and frankly I've been making homophobes more heavenly.

I mean,
I don't believe in all that god stuff but I still hoped there was
something up there, keeping people safe.
Maybe I'm that now.
I don't know, but this feels

good
more than bad
if I'm honest.
Palpable power in the palm of my hand,
some sense of control in the universe.
When I walk now, my strides have godly intent.

I will do no harm.
Only protect.
I will make this reckoning the very softest yet. //

Buttercup

All the monsters, they've all gone to bed now.
Tucked them under blankets, kissed their foreheads.
Fed them milk. Told them stories -
the ones from ancient times.

Everyone is safe now,
warm now,
kind now.
Isn't that nice?
Isn't that better?
I am going to *keep* making the world better.
Then after,
we can live happily together,
playing in perfect princess houses.
Well-trimmed hedges, fruit-filled gardens,
Idyllic Eden.

Just like it should be.
I'll make everything like it should be.
No more apocalypse or the need to sing sad songs.
I'm going to change the tune and make them sing
along.

Can't you picture it?
Strawberry flavoured rivers and all the witches
growing turnips,
hordes of butterflies perched on petal edge.
Nobody broken, nobody sad
ever again.

Isn't it nice?
Tell me it's pretty.
I'm painting this picture for you.

Pam II

"Hey. Sorry I bailed
the other day, it was
surreal really, I mean–"

                                            "It's fine."

"No, it really
isn't though.
Look Pam, I like you.
I mean, I really like you–"

                        "You should've called then."

"Please, just
let me explain."

A silent beat, then:

                                "Alright, sit down.
                                  Want a drink?"

"No, I–"

                                "Give me a second.
                                I do. Back in a sec."

I watch her disappear through the doorway.
When she returns, lipstick smeared wine glass in
hand, she looks
dejected, tired, hasn't slept, still
beautiful somehow. Anyway, don't think about that.
Be present.
She deserves your presence. She deserves
everything.

"You were going to explain."

"Yes. Of course."
I start to fidget,
wring my hands nervously.
Emotions are shards, but I
want to piece them together,
want to share them with her.
I think I know what this feeling is.

"Thing is,
I don't know if you'll even believe me.
But my scramble suit heart, well, it thinks you ought to know.
The night you mean, a closing cafe, something scary, and then,
well, god, *how* do you explain?
Then something changed me.
I don't know what.
Maybe being caught there again, frozen fury, a trigger,
either way, I blacked out and woke up later that day all
covered in bruises, and I thought I'd killed a man but I didn't,
I just changed him, I don't know how it works, I have people
working on it in my head. Does any of this even make sense?"

"Not really."

"Right."
I wring my hands again.

"It doesn't make much to me either, but I need you to believe me, you see,
I would never have left you, would *never* have ignored you, if it weren't for
Alice and the vanishing house and the blackouts and the tiny not-me versions of me who somehow control aspects of our universe in a way I don't really get a say in but can somehow
control now
by the way."

She looks me up and down.
I can see it on her face, her cynic's eyebrow, cold appraisal.
This is not going in my favour.
I need a saviour.

"I've told Kyle and Marie.
You can ask them if you want.
Or I can show you—"

> "Thanks, but I don't think I want to. Ev, come on. I think I deserve a lie that's at least better constructed."

"It's no lie. I promise."

> "Then maybe you should phone a doctor. Has anyone *else* seen this magic vanishing house?"

"Well, no. It only exists there sometimes,
it's a whole space time thing there's little time to get into."

> "Seems convenient."

"Not really, no.
I mean it Pam, all of this *is* real."

                    "I'm more than sceptical."

"I'm getting that.
And frankly, there's every reason to be.
But whatever's happening to me is, well, *happening* to me.
I really wouldn't lie to you. Pam, please believe–"

                    "I think you should leave."

This last request a bullet ricocheting against my
eardrum, a physical sting, a rejection, banshee
scream, bursting brain cells in the bleak silence of it
all
and then

something happens.
The world does not drop out from under me, but
I lose control, watch in terror, as my body becomes
something else,
my greatest traitor.

I begin the dance, fighting with every step.

I watch the product of my bloodsport change her face.
Creases where there weren't, broken down eyes still
bright but
different, starkly different, I can see it.
Cannot look as my limbs move without my beckoning.
Seven figures all about us.
Dancing, fluid motion, serene and somehow
panicked, frantic, frightened.

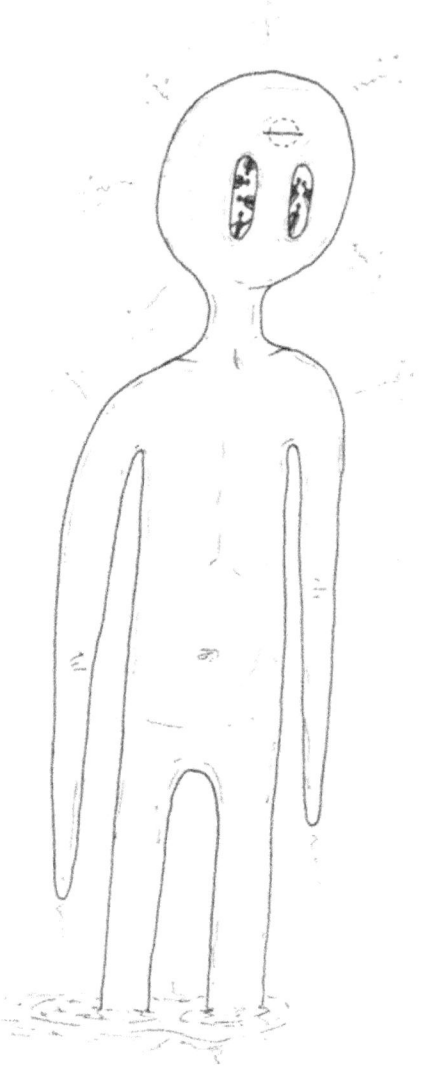

Stop this.
I don't want this.
Not now.

I smell the strawberries. See the gold dust.
What have I *done?*

Pathetic, far too cowardly,
I run. ⫽

Mother Mary

You've been staring at the sun a little long, pet.
Think it's given you a different walk, a different look.
You don't smile so easy anymore, why not?

I mean, I know why not.
Try not to dwell on it.
Come here. Don't fret.
I'll look after you.

Be your mentor and your martyr.
I'll cook the vegetables, make the decisions,
clean up all the blood.

I am not here for pious judgement, but I gift you my
holiness if it helps.

Settle down now.
There's no need to be worried.
I'm going to fix it.
I always fix it.
I will be your castle now.
Get some rest.

These reckonings grew a little less than blessed, but
everything will be better by the morning. ⁄⁄

Changing Minds

Buzzer noise. Morning after. You know the scene.
Waiting. A small infinity of waiting, then
crackly voice, asks who is it, lets me in.
I grip the bannister, ascend cautiously, terrified but I
continue heavenward   *Man, I don't feel it.*
toward her halo   *I can't heal this.*
and   *Who am I to even try?*

she's just, standing there.
One hand in her pocket, gentle eyes, wide smile,
ready to greet me, coffee in hand.
I don't deserve this.
"Hi Pam,
how are you?"

She says good. Funny though.
And would I like anything?
There's rolls in the kitchen, she can cook up
something.
I look hungry, and she knows I never remember
breakfast.
I ask her if she remembers last night.

      "Oh, you mean our fight? Yeah, I mean, kinda.
           Honestly, it is a little fuzzy."

She shrugs. *She's lovely.*

      "Anyway, sorry I got upset.
        Little cranky I guess.
    Glad you came over though, I
        think we need to talk."

I knew it. Something's different, I can sense it.
I know almost *exactly* what I did.

"See, the thing is,
I guess I've been getting ahead of myself,
leading you on a bit. To tell the truth, I'm suddenly
not that into this. I can't quite
explain it. Just this feeling in my stomach,
like suddenly I feel like a brand new person
and I don't think *this* works with that."

She raises her palms. I feel stigmatas in my own.

"It's not like you've done anything wrong.
There's just this ringing in my gut, you know?
A changing. Something new.
And I think it's going in a different direction to you.
I'm sorry.
I know all this seems sudden."

My cheeks burn hotter than an oven
but I stand, resolute, try not to react.
"If that's what you want."

"I think that I do."

"Well then. I'll be on my way." ⁄⁄

Friendship Insert

After the first few heartbreaks, you develop a system:
cry, talk, drink, dance, fuck.
Take up new hobby if unsuccessful.
Drown out feelings with loud music.
Rinse, lather, repeat until they are washed out of your hair.
Dependable.
Straightforward.
Simple.

Less so when the reason for said heartbreak seems to be your inability to regulate the psychology-altering microverse somehow synchronised to your panic responses.
Less so when your (ex)girlfriend doesn't believe any of this could be possible, so trying to explain this to her seems a little useless.

I need help.
I rush home.
I'm done dealing with all this alone.

I bang on Kyle's bedroom door til my fists are sore.
He meets me groggy-eyed, pinstripe dressing gown prepared.
We call Marie and within ten minutes, she's there.
I explain everything hastily, answer their questions, watch their shoulders tense.
Marie grabs my hand, squeezes, and I take a breath.

"First thing's first," she says. "*Can* you undo it?"

"Shit, I don't know.
If I can, I will of course,
but this is all still so new."

"Wasn't there someone," Kyle yawns, "at that weird house,
who might know what do so?" ⌇

Looking Glass

"Can I undo it?"
I am staring desperately across the table at Alice, its
marble surface glistening
> *wait, wasn't this made of wood the
> time before?*
> *No time for that.*

"Alice, please. Can't you see that I really need to
know?
I need to fix this. It's my mess, I never wanted it to all
end up like *this*."
I glance sideways at my mirror image, distrusting.
Hope that they aren't listening.

"I'm afraid I do not know.
If I did, of course I'd tell you.
But my own curse works in a very different way,
and I am afraid the others are, well, much the same.
I fear the only answer for this–"

"Lies in my own brain, I figured, fuck, thanks
anyway."
I cut her off.
Remind myself to apologise for that later,
feel the rock in my pocket, stalwart centring,
turn to Kyle and Marie.

"Things are about to get
a little weird." ⁂

Panoplay II

Evelyn: *[shouting]*   Hello! Hi. We have a *big* problem.

[Biter rolls her eyes and grunts]

Mother Mary: We know that, sweetie.

Evelyn: Well? What are we going to *do* about it? Come on.

Biter: Bitter about being single, are we?

Evelyn: *No. [A pause]* Yes. Maybe a little. But it's more than that. Something about this doesn't feel... *right.*

Biter: Felt fine before though, did it?

Mother Mary: Don't try to antagonise her.

Rebel Girl: She's got a point though. I don't like what we did to Pam. It gives me... I don't know, a bad feeling.

Buttercup: I miss her.

Brightspark: Me too. She was so fun. But! Onto the next, hm?

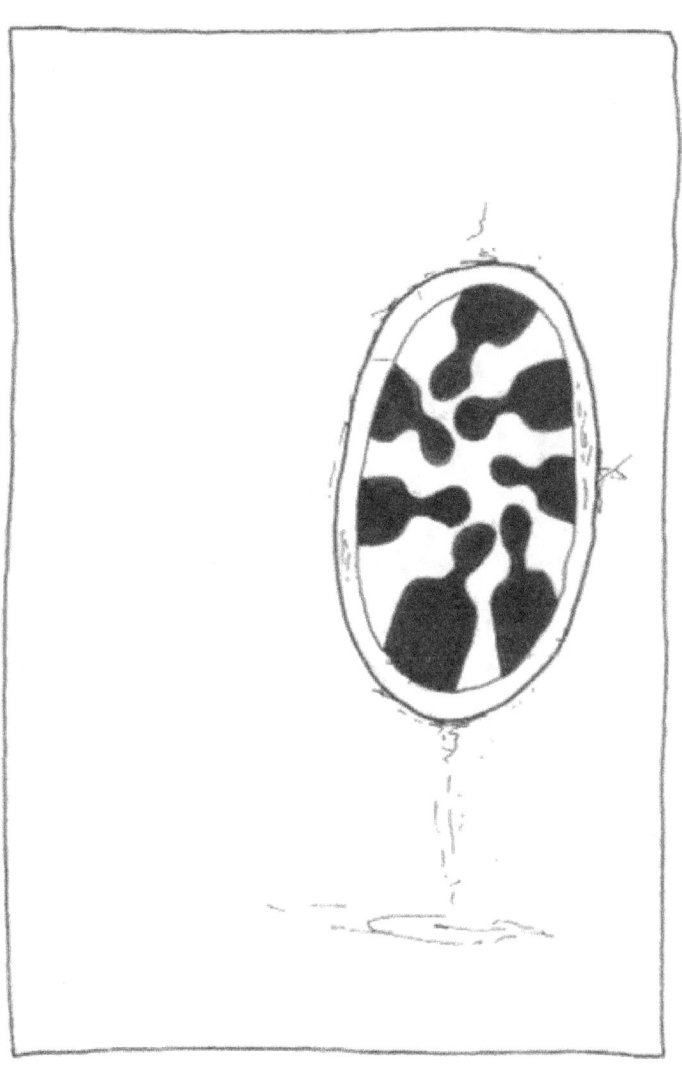

Evelyn: What? No, that's not... Look, *sure*, Pam breaking up with me of her own accord and free will would be very, *very* unpleasant, but this... I did this. *We* did this. I need to, I don't know, fix it, make it better, do *something*. Whatever this thing is, this weird 'correcting' power, why did it zone in on our relationship, why did it... *erase* those feelings? That isn't *life*, that isn't Pam, it's just...

Brightspark: Too specific?

Rebel Girl: A little dramatic?

Biter: Self-absorbed, pig-headed and arrogant?

Mother Mary: *[frowning]* I don't think that's appropriate.

[Evelyn looks up, eyes wide with realisation]

Evelyn: No, she's right, it's... If you're all tied to me, and this power thing is, you know, tied *to me*, then it doesn't seem *ridiculous* to think that maybe the way it works, it's something to do with *my* perceptions of things. What I think is a flaw, or whatever, is the thing it zones in on. I mean, I guess I figured it was *something* like that, sort of... I don't know. I don't know what I thought. I just know I want rid of this. I want to be better already. I want to know what you know. So. *Tell me.*

[All seven are silent for a long moment. Evelyn taps her foot impatiently]

Evelyn: I'm sorry, to be clear, time *is* of the essence here. I want *answers.*

Prophet: Answers, answers. Always looking for the wrong ones.

Evelyn: What's that supposed to mean?

[Prophet remains silent, almost motionless]

Evelyn: You know, ambiguity really isn't helping. *[to Lauren]* You. I did what you asked. What do you have for me?

[Lauren clears her throat, looking nervously at the floor]

Lauren: Research has been, *ah*, less helpful than previously hoped. Or more. Maybe? No. *[She shakes her head]* Definitely less.

Evelyn: What's *that* supposed to mean? Are you telling me I did all this for *nothing*?

Lauren: Not nothing exactly, just... Um, the complexity of the situation... I was so sure before of everything, of what I was at least but–

Evelyn: *Today*, please.

Lauren: It seems we're um, connected to some sort of signal. Probably sprung from it, actually. A bit like a parasite or nanogene or–

Evelyn: A... signal?

Biter: That's what she said.

Lauren: Yes, something, we're not sure what, is emitting a sort of biochemical wave, which has latched onto you, causing us, and you, to be like, well, *this*. Creating us. Creating your ability. The

	technology for it is so complicated, far beyond what I can decipher or even really *determine* beyond the signal's origin.
Evelyn:	But you've determined the origin?
Lauren:	Yes.
Evelyn:	Who?
Lauren:	I only have the location, but...
Evelyn:	*Where?* ⁄⁄

Traversing the Universe

Space is not so daunting as they describe it.
Of course, the emptiness echoes for eons, but
it's quiet,
the stars are pretty,
I feel at peace.
Well,
relatively.

I am gritted teeth wonder as the planet passes by,
its marble surface, so much more blue than I
imagined,
pales in comparison to the wavelengths of green and
violet light
weaving a web of fate almost galaxy-wide.
Kaleidoscopes of colour.
They should have sent a poet.
I am struck with awe, dumbfounded but

not alone.

Marie wipes the sweat from her brow with the back of
her hand,
smiles, panting, and says she found supplies in the
back.
Kyle grins widely, says "We'll be there in a minute or
two."

Flash forward past boarding and hesitance,
past fear of the unknown, onto adventure, onto
danger,
onto something that makes *sense*.

Beat the bad guy, save the world, go home with my friends.
Maybe even get the girl back
if I'm lucky.

I get to the door and I am *ready*, you know?
Adrenaline drunk and ragin'.
Flooded with red-handed righteousness.
Who the fuck *do you even think you are?*

But the creature in the centre of the room is small,
green and shivering,
curled in on itself, a wet, sobbing slug,
and I drop my weapon almost
instantly.

I suppose this isn't that kind of story.

I sit down, cross legged, next to it on the floor.
It seems frightened, though seemingly not of me.
I ask softly if it is the thing who made me like this,
distorted by my own mirror image.
It nods, I swallow.
"Okay then.
I think I have some questions." ⧘

Why

Its voice is exposed nerve, warbling reply:

"I am the thing that wrenched you up out of the water.
Dragged your bleeding fingernails over riverbeds until they grew to rock, grew to mountain,
and still I pulled you up.
That small knot in your stomach that makes you stay alive,
keep fighting, burn brighter in spite of every weight on your back,
that's me.
I mean,
I am a visitor from a faraway galaxy,
this definitely isn't a metaphor.
Scratch that, start over.

My name won't translate, but
I promise I'm a friend.
Or at least, I'm trying to be.
I saw the pain in your eyes from a million miles away
and gods, I couldn't bear it.
I've felt the screaming, felt the madness, still struggle with peace.
But you, still that glimmer in your eye.
I had to protect it. Protect *you*.
I might've overstepped,
but your heart was so full of anguish, I couldn't stand it,
and I'm sorry that my radar was a little off.
I gave you the tools my people gave me,
persuasion, survival, dissolve the fragments,
I had *nothing* else.

Should've known that what I come from is hell, and you live
something different now."

"Not all the time."

"Yes," it tries to laugh.
"But things are softer now.
You're outgrowing me and the world is not so dark,
not all the time either. I worry
that I am lately of little use.
And that's... *fine*.
The way of things, only right.
I've done more harm than good, but
all I wanted was to see you safe enough to grow
and look at all the petals you've been sprouting lately.
They're amazing.
I'm only glad I got to live this long and see them.

It is right that I go,
but allow me to pray this apology makes redemption.
I am sorry, my friend.
I'm sorry there's nothing I can do but say
sorry.
I only meant to help.
I saw you frightened, saw you alone,
simply needed you *safe*.
I need you to understand that.
I didn't know what else to do.
But I had to do something, could not
simply leave you.

There may be chaos in the universe, but there is also us." ⁄⁄

Hugging an Alien

I hear that last part and it makes me hesitate.
So ready to unburden my rage, my anger,
and for what? Brief catharsis, shattered dream,
to grasp at something bordering on sense in a
universe mostly unburdened by it.
What's the *point?*
In all this burning, all this confusion.
It's so hard to say. There might not be any.
I should be shouting now, one long guttural scream,
and yet

I'm not.
In fact, you could hear a pin drop,
this weighted silence, not the kind that makes the
skin rot, just
one in waiting.

I decide to fill it.

"You saw pain from across the stars and answered it.
Took all the sorrow I couldn't swallow and made it
settle.
Made me feel powerful in a world that'd broken me
down
again
and again
and again.
Tell me, how could I leave you now?
With your broken shards across the floor, denied
sweet mortal empathy,
No I'm sorry, you mustn't know me well at all.
I'm a broken bird too, don't you know?
Often/always misconstruction, shambles of a girl,

could never claim that my pain's never had its side
effects –
albeit admittedly, nothing quite like this."
Brief pause.
"My point is
I'm all sorts of fucked up too,
just trying to to gather something good together from
the dust,
so I'm finding it impossible to forsake you.

I can't imagine the strength it took to come this far,
to be so alone yet give so much, you are
so *brave*. I want to help you too
in whatever way I can.

We are not so different, you and I.
Not so estranged by space's chasm.
And maybe supernovas all look the same to some, but
you and I, a fragile wonder, curiosity and love
slicing through the fear. That
still matters, must matter.
After all,
the best thing we can do in this life is make each other
feel less lonely.

It won't be easy,
but we'll meet it hand in hand at least.
Trust me.
Everything'll be okay.
Come home with us." ⁄⁄

Prophet

We settle into our new normal graciously.
Unpack boxes, put up string lights, even paint.
Get a tank for our new alien friend.
Visit the mirror on Wednesdays.
Dinner every Sunday. Folding up the laundry.
Trying our *best*.

Put Pam through a series of tests, try to
undo my damage.
Five heads are better than one,
or any other familiar adage.
It's slow going, but
at least she believes me now.

We're getting there.

Sleeping through the night again.
Trying to be present. Keeping my cool.
Doing my best to prevent another shatter.

Where we were, who we've been, that doesn't matter.

The important thing to note is
this is not an ending. ⁄⁄

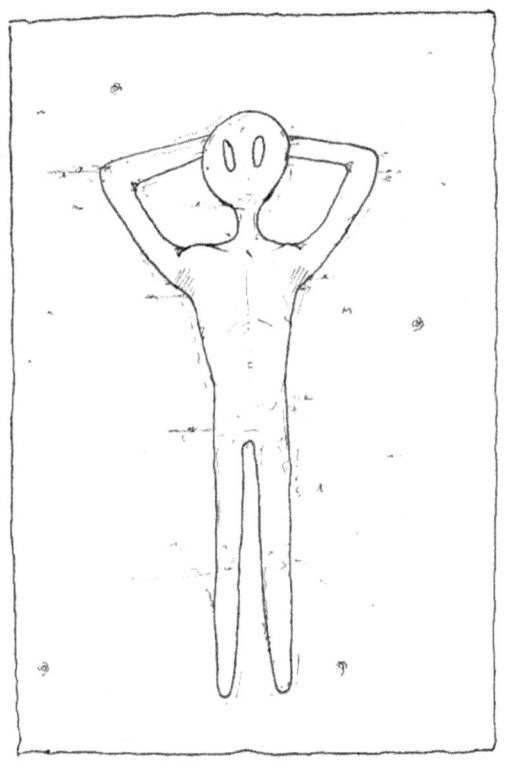

Acknowledgements

No man is an island, and similarly no completed work of any artistic merit comes from simply one individual's efforts. I wrote it, true, but there were many people who facilitated its writing, who read and helped me figure out what it would look like, and to whom I arguably owe the form of my artistic career as it is now. This list is not exhaustive by any means, but indicates some of the people I think thanks are owed to. If I have forgotten you, I'm afraid I'm only human.

First and foremost, there is, as with so many writers, my partner, Mark, who has stayed up so many nights listening to my rantings about plot structure that I feel he deserves an award. Similar gratitude should be extended to a flurry of my friends, not least among them the wonderful Jade Mitchell and Ross Hunter, who I think took most of the more fervent ranting when Mark wasn't around. Thanks to Tyrone, Imogen and Texture, for the quotes, the friendship and being patient with my panicked emails, and to the Glasgow arts scene for facilitating me all these years. Thanks to Bethany Sanderson for letting me run rogue with a microphone whenever I wanted (you truly are the best among co-hosts), and to everyone who attended Aloud in the years we ran it, because I don't think I could have built this kind of confidence (or arrogance) without you. Thank you to my family for always daring me to dream big, but especially to my sisters, for their unending kindness and inspiration. Thank you to Mort Johnstone, for the free coffee, and to Phyllis for the ongoing support. Thank you to In The Works, for giving me a stage and space to blend my loves of poetry and theatre. And, of course, thank you to Rose Drew, Tanya, Alan and everyone at Stairwell Books – they are very much the reason you're reading this right now, and I really couldn't have asked for more understanding and dedicated publishers.

Other anthologies and collections available from Stairwell Books

Unknown	Anna Rose James and Elizabeth Chadwick Pywell
When We Wake We Think We're Whalers from Eden	Bob Beagrie
Awakening	Richard Harries
Geography Is Irrelevant	Ed. Rose Drew and Amina Alyal, Raef Boylan
Belong	Ed. Verity Glendenning and Stephanie Venn, Amy E Creighton
Starspin	Grahaeme Barrasford Young
Out of the Dreaming Dark	F. Mary Callan and Joy Simpson
A Stray Dog, Following	Greg Quiery
Blue Saxophone	Rosemary Palmeira
Waiting at the Temporary Traffic Lights	Graham Lee
Steel Tipped Snowflakes 1	Izzy Rhiannon Jones, Becca Miles, Laura Voivodeship
Where the Hares Are	John Gilham
Something I Need to Tell You	William Thirsk-Gaskill
The Glass King	Gary Allen
The River Was a God	David Lee Morgan
A Thing of Beauty Is a Joy Forever	Don Walls
Gooseberries	Val Horner
Poetry for the Newly Single 40 Something	Maria Stephenson
Northern Lights	Harry Gallagher
Nothing Is Meant to be Broken	Mark Connors
Heading for the Hills	Gillian Byrom-Smith
More Exhibitionism	Ed. Glen Taylor
Rhinoceros	Daniel Richardson
The Beggars of York	Don Walls
Lodestone	Hannah Stone
Unsettled Accounts	Tony Lucas
Learning to Breathe	John Gilham
The Problem with Beauty	Tanya Nightingale
New Crops from Old Fields	Ed. Oz Hardwick
The Ordinariness of Parrots	Amina Alyal
Homeless	Ed. Ross Raisin
Sometimes I Fly	Tim Goldthorpe
Somewhere Else	Don Walls
Still Life with Wine and Cheese	Ed. Rose Drew and Alan Gillott
Skydive	Andrew Brown
Taking the Long Way Home	Steve Nash
York in Poetry Artwork and Photographs	Ed. John Coopey and Sally Guthrie

For further information please contact rose@stairwellbooks.com
www.stairwellbooks.co.uk
@stairwellbooks

www.ingramcontent.com/pod-product-compliance
Lightning Source LLC
LaVergne TN
LVHW051604080426
835510LV00020B/3121